Travel Fun
Activity Book

Fran Newman-D'Amico

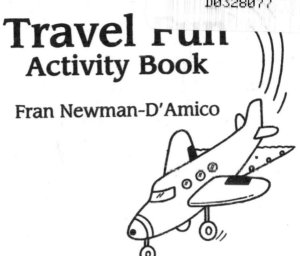

DOVER PUBLICATIONS, INC.
Mineola, New York

Copyright

Copyright © 2004 by Dover Publications, Inc.
All rights reserved.

Bibliographical Note

Travel Fun Activity Book is a new work, first published by Dover
Publications, Inc., in 2004.

International Standard Book Number: 0-486-43532-6

Manufactured in the United States of America
Dover Publications, Inc., 31 East 2nd Street, Mineola, N.Y. 11501

Note

Have you ever sat in a car, or on a bus, plane, or train, and wondered how to make the time go by? This little book will keep you busy! It is full of puzzles such as mazes, crosswords, follow-the-dots, find the differences, word searches, and more. Whether you are going on vacation, or taking a short ride to Grandma and Grandpa's, you can have a good time on the way. Make sure to take a pencil and crayons with you. When you have finished the puzzles, you can have even more fun coloring in the pages!

Finish packing for your vacation! Circle the four
things that will go in the suitcase.

Dear _____ ,

I am at _____ .

I can _____ .

I am having _____

Mom

the beach

Grandma's

Dad

swim

a good time

play

fun

Fill in this postcard. Pick one word or group of
words to go in each sentence.

5

Airports are busy places. Here are some planes taking off and landing. Circle the planes that are taking off.

6

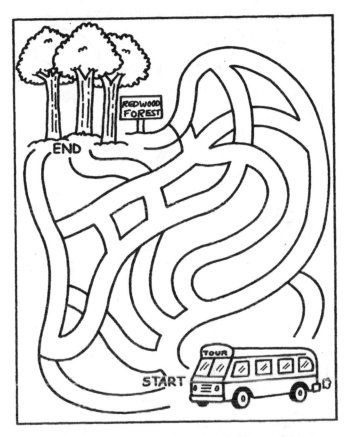

This bus is taking people to the Redwood Forest.
Help the bus find its way through the maze.

When it is 5 o'clock in New York, it is three hours earlier in California. Make the bottom watch show the time in California.

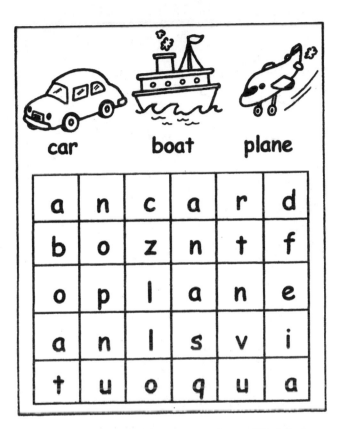

car   boat   plane

a	n	c	a	r	d
b	o	z	n	t	f
o	p	l	a	n	e
a	n	l	s	v	i
t	u	o	q	u	a

We may use these things to go places. Find their
names in the puzzle and circle them.

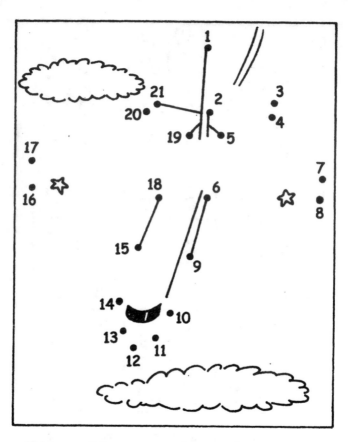

Take one of these to go to faraway places. Connect the dots to see its picture.

Your pilot is waving to you. He is the one with the striped tie and sunglasses. Circle his picture.

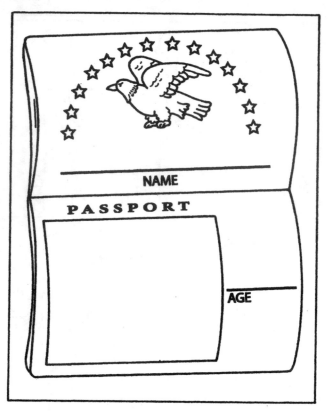

NAME

PASSPORT

AGE

Here is your passport. Draw a small picture of your
face in the space. Then fill in your name and age.
Now you're ready to go!

Send a friend this postcard of the Eiffel Tower in Paris. Color **1** dark green, **2** light green, **3** blue, **4** gray, **5** yellow, and **6** white.

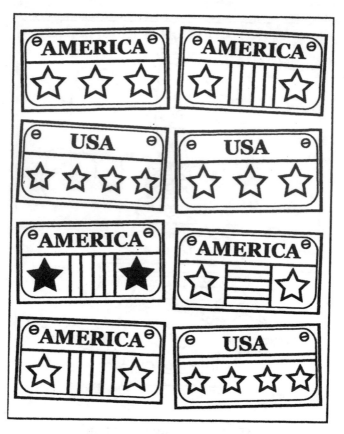

It's fun to look at license plates when you travel by car. Circle the two license plates that are exactly alike.

14

What can run and whistle, but can't walk or talk ?

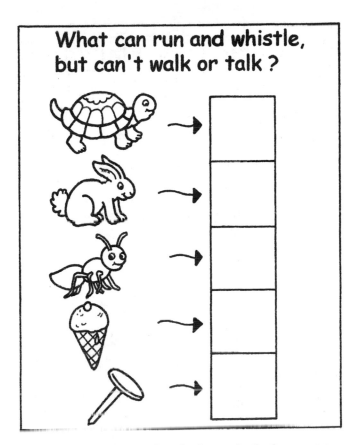

Write the first letter of each picture in the box next to it. Then you will spell out the answer to the riddle!

Let's camp out on the mountain! The first word in the puzzle has been done for you. Use the pictures on the opposite page to solve the rest of the puzzle.

2.

3. down

4. down

5.

The number next to each picture tells you where the word belongs in the puzzle.

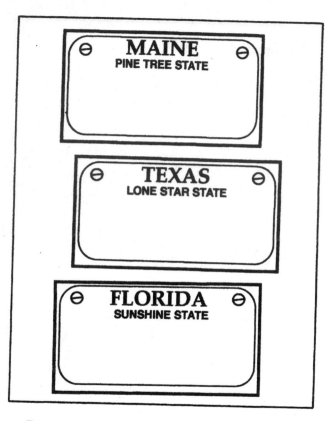

Draw a picture on each license plate. The words
under the state names will give you clues
about what picture to use.

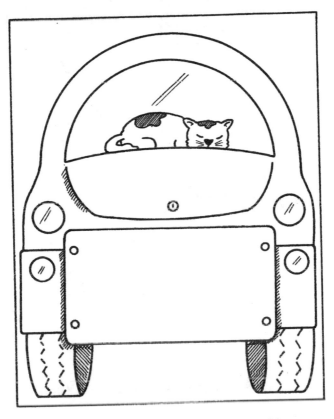

Draw a picture of what you think should go
on your license plate.

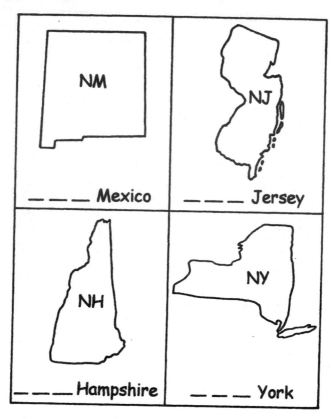

NM _ _ _ Mexico	NJ _ _ _ Jersey
NH _ _ _ Hampshire	NY _ _ _ York

The first word in the name of each of these states
is the same. Guess the word and then
write it in on the blanks.

Look out of this train window. Put an X on the
shortest mountain. Circle the tallest mountain.

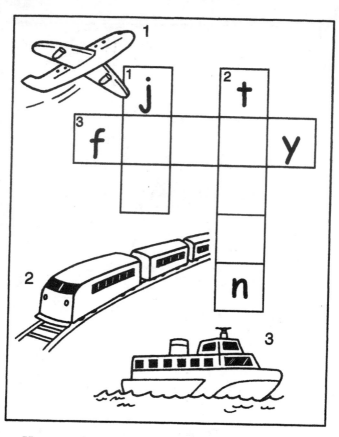

Here are pictures of three different ways to travel.
Fill in the puzzle with their names.

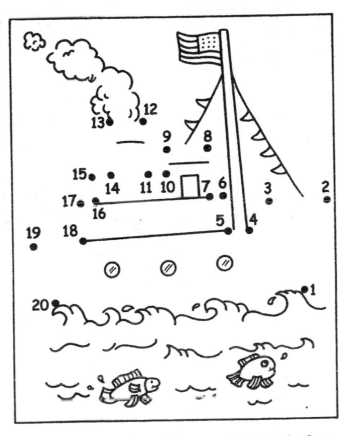

This will take you across the ocean. Connect the dots from 1 to 20 to see what it is.

This plane has just landed on the airport runway.

This picture looks the same, but five things have changed. Find the changes and circle them.

In the middle of this picture is a suspension bridge.
Connect the dots from 1 to 15 to see the bridge.

26

Find the path so that this car can reach the top of the highest mountain.

Which town would Lindsay reach first? Shade in the
sign. Which town would she reach last?
Circle the sign.

What kind of tie can't you wear? Use the code at the top to fill in the blanks and solve the riddle!

Let's visit this farmer and his stand.

That's funny! The picture has changed! Find and circle the five things that are different.

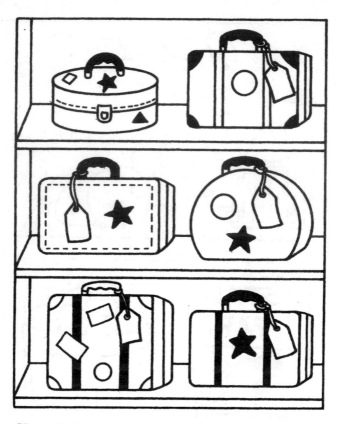

Your missing suitcase has turned up in the Lost and
Found. It's the one with two stripes,
a star, and a tag. Circle it.

Get ready for your ski trip! Circle the things that you will bring. Cross out the rest.

The name of this famous clock tower in England is
spelled backwards. Write the letters in the
reverse order to spell the name.

It's a fine day for a fishing trip! Circle the two fish
whose numbers added together make 10.

Here are some things you might see at a park. Draw a line from the creature or thing on the left to the word it rhymes with on the right.

Connect the dots from 1 to 20 to see what is coming out of the tunnel. It's fun to take a ride on one of these!

END

START

Carmen has lost her way! Help her find the
path to get to her tent.

Signs help people stay safe when they travel. Find the
two signs that are exactly alike and circle them.

Let's spend the day at the beach! It's warm and
sunny, and the water is so inviting!

40

The first word in the puzzle has been done for you.
Use the picture clues to solve the rest of the puzzle.

What sits in a corner while traveling all around the world?

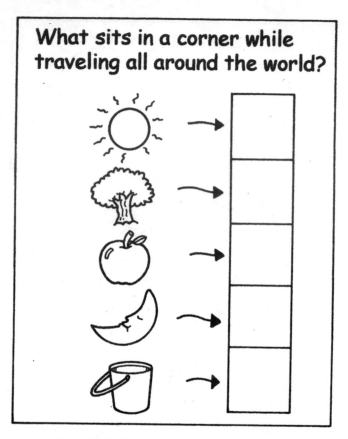

Solve this riddle by writing the first letter of each picture in the box.

bus   tag   pilot

a	p	c	z	e	d
b	i	a	t	a	g
o	l	f	o	w	e
r	o	b	u	s	l
u	t	o	q	p	a

Here are some travel words. Find all three of them in
the puzzle and circle them. Look down and across.

Leroy is excited about hiking through the forest.
He's packed and ready to go!

44

This picture is different. Five things have changed.
Find and circle all five things.

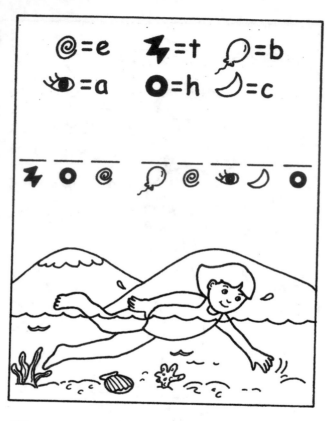

Where can you go swimming on your vacation? Use
the code at the top to write the letters
in the blanks. Now you know!

The airline flight attendant is holding the snack tray.
Draw in two or three other snacks
that are good to eat.

This cruise ship is sailing over the ocean. Find and circle the two ships that are exactly the same.

What things should Tina take on her camping trip?
Circle them. Then cross out the rest.

E B O L G

‾ ‾ ‾ ‾ ‾

The name of this object is written backwards. Write
the letters in reverse to find out what this
round map of the world is called.

Write yes in the box of the picture that shows
your favorite season to be outdoors.
Put an x in the other box.

Solutions

page 4

Dear __Mom, Dad__ ,

I am at __Grandma's, the beach__

I can __swim , play__

I am having __a good time, fun__

Mom	the beach
Grandma's	Dad
swim	a good time
play	fun

page 5

page 6

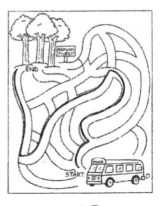

page 7

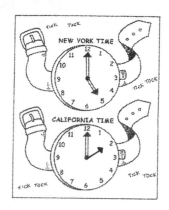

page 8

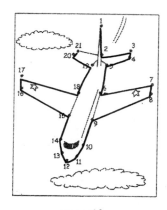

page 10

a	n	c	a	r	d
b	o	z	n	t	f
o	p	l	a	n	e
a	n	l	s	v	i
t	u	o	q	u	a

page 9

page 11

page 14

What can run and whistle,
but can't walk or talk?

t
r
a
i
n

page 15

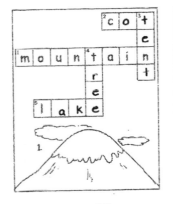

page 16

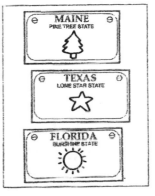

MAINE
PINE TREE STATE

TEXAS
LONE STAR STATE

FLORIDA
SUNSHINE STATE

page 18

page 20

page 21

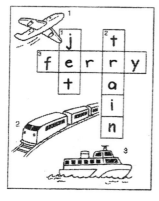

page 22

page 23

page 25

page 26

page 27

page 28

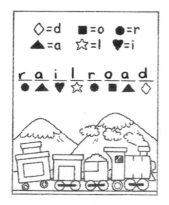

page 29

page 31

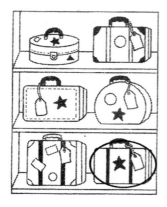

page 32

page 33

page 34

page 35

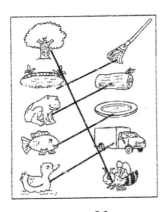

page 36

page 37

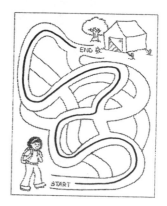

page 38

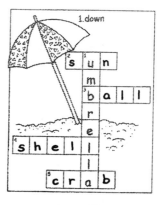

STOP GO STOP Stop GO GO STOP STOP

page 39

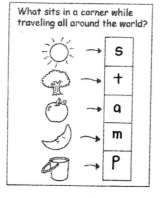

1.down

s u n
m
b a l l
r
e
s h e l l
l
c r a b

page 40

What sits in a corner while traveling all around the world?

S t a m p

page 42

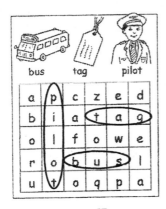

page 43

page 45

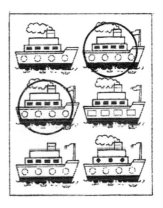

page 46

page 48

page 49

page 50

page 51